Contents

Words in **bold** are in the glossary on page 30.

What is Easter?

Easter is celebrated every year by millions of people all over the world. But what is Easter and why do we celebrate it?

The first Easter

Easter is the most important time in the **Christian** year. The day that Jesus was put to death on a cross is called **Good Friday**. Christians believe that Jesus came back to life again two days later. This was the first Easter. It is celebrated on Easter Sunday.

Pre-Christian celebrations

In the **northern hemisphere**, Easter usually falls at the beginning of spring. But long before Jesus Christ, people celebrated the arrival of spring after the cold, dark days of winter. Many Easter traditions come from these ancient springtime festivals.

People celebrate Easter in different ways around the world. What do you enjoy the most at Easter?

Eating chocolate eggs?

Hunting for Easter eggs?

Wearing Easter bonnets?

The Easter story

Jesus had been spreading God's word in towns and villages all over **Palestine**. Many people loved him but others did not like him, or the words he spoke.

Jesus and his twelve **disciples** went to Jerusalem for the Jewish feast of **Passover**. Jesus had many enemies in Jerusalem. He knew they would kill him. On the way Jesus warned his disciples that he would soon die.

Some people believed that God would one day send a new King of the Jews. They said he would enter Jerusalem on a donkey.

Jesus borrowed a donkey and rode on it into Jerusalem. The crowds shouted "Jesus is King!" They threw **palm** leaves down in front of Jesus.

Some of the **priests** were unhappy that Jesus was so popular. They offered Judas, one of the disciples, thirty pieces of silver to betray his friend. Judas took the money.

Later that week Jesus and his twelve disciples sat down for a meal together. Jesus told them that one of the disciples had already taken money to betray him. He explained that he would be **arrested** and killed. But he told the disciples not to be sad because he was going to **heaven** to be with God.

That night Jesus went with some of the disciples to the Garden of Gethsemane to pray. In the early morning, Judas arrived with guards and soldiers. The guards arrested Jesus and took him to Pontius Pilate, the Roman leader. He was tried and sentenced to death.

Jesus was given a crown of sharp thorns to wear on his head. He was made to drag a large wooden cross to the top of a nearby hill. The soldiers nailed Jesus to the cross and raised it up with a sign saying, 'The King of the Jews'.

That night Jesus died. Jesus's friends took his body and laid it in a **tomb**. They rolled a heavy stone across the entrance to seal the tomb.

This stone tomb is like the one that Jesus was laid in on the night he died.

Two days later a friend of Jesus called Mary Magdalen went to visit the tomb. When she got there she found that the stone had been rolled away from the entrance. Inside there was no sign of Jesus's body.

As Mary stood alone, crying, Jesus appeared before her and spoke to her. Mary told the disciples what had happened, but at first they did not believe her.

Then Jesus appeared to the disciples. He told them. "Go into the world, and preach the **gospel** to everyone." Later, Jesus went up to heaven to be with God.

Shrove Tuesday

Shrove Tuesday is the day before **Lent.** Lent is the important run up to Easter (see pages 14–15). In the past, many people did not eat meat, eggs, sugar and butter during Lent. Today, some people give up treats like chocolate instead.

Shrove Tuesday was the day when people held feasts to use up all the food they were not going to eat during Lent.

These are some of the delicious treats people still make on Shrove Tuesday.

Poland – paczki doughnuts fried in oil

Australia – thick pancakes served cold with cream and jam

Canada – pancakes served with sausages and jam

Great Britain – pancakes served with lemon and sugar

Sweden – round buns filled with marzipan and thick cream

Celebrations

In many parts of the world there are spectacular celebrations on Shrove Tuesday.

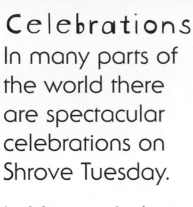

In Venice, Italy, people wear crazy carnival masks. There are parades and street theatre performances.

In some places Shrove Tuesday is called **Mardi Gras**. In cities such as New Orleans, in the USA, and Rio de Janeiro, in Brazil there are big Mardi Gras parades. Millions of people go to watch the decorated **floats**, to dance and have fun.

11

How to make
pancakes

Shrove Tuesday is sometimes called 'pancake day'. In the past people made pancakes to use up all their eggs, sugar and butter before Lent. Pancakes are made in a very hot pan, so ask an adult to cook them for you.

You will need:
* bowl, whisk and cup
* 110g plain flour
* pinch of salt
* 1 egg
* 275ml milk
* frying pan and fish slice
* butter for frying
* plate
! Hot fat is very dangerous
  – ask a grown-up to help

Instructions

1 Sift the flour and salt into a bowl.

2 Crack the egg into a cup. Make a hole in the centre of the flour and pour in the egg.

3 Add a little of the milk and mix well with a hand whisk. Add the rest of the milk gradually, whisking all the time.

Ask an adult to do steps 4–7 while you prepare the fillings.

4 Add a little piece of butter to a hot frying pan. Pour in 2 to 3 tablespoons of the mixture.

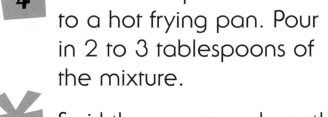

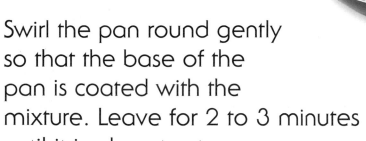

5 Swirl the pan round gently so that the base of the pan is coated with the mixture. Leave for 2 to 3 minutes until it is almost set.

6 Flip the pancake over with a fish slice. Cook for a further 2 to 3 minutes.

7 Slide the pancake out on to a plate.

Pancake fillings

Pancakes are tasty served simply with a squeeze of lemon juice and a sprinkle of sugar. But there are lots of other ways to enjoy pancakes. Try these yummy fillings:

* raspberries and ice cream with a drizzle of raspberry sauce

* sliced banana and ice cream

* banana and maple syrup

All about Lent

The time leading up to Easter is called Lent.

Forty days

The traditions of Lent come from the forty days that Jesus spent in the desert, praying and preparing to do God's work. During that time he did not eat. Some people try to follow his example and give up treats during the forty days of Lent.

Ash Wednesday

The first day of Lent is called **Ash Wednesday**. In some churches, the priest makes the mark of a cross on each person's forehead with ash. The ash comes from burned **palm crosses** from the previous year. The ash crosses are signs that people are sorry for things they have done wrong in the past year.

Palm Sunday

The last week of Lent, leading up to Easter, is called **Holy Week**. It starts with **Palm Sunday**. On this day, Christians carry a cross made from the leaves of a palm tree. The cross celebrates Jesus's arrival in Jerusalem on a donkey, when the crowds laid down palm leaves in front of him.

Good Friday

On Good Friday, Christians all over the world remember Jesus's death on the cross. Many people go to church services to reflect on the **crucifixion**.

It is traditional to eat hot cross buns on Good Friday. These are spicy buns with a pastry cross on the top. The buns remind people of the cross on which Jesus was crucified.

Easter Sunday

Easter Sunday is one of the two most important days for Christians (the other is Christmas Day). Easter Sunday is a very happy day when they remember that Jesus came back from the dead (the **resurrection**). Christians all over the world attend special church services.

Sunrise service

Some Christians take part in a sunrise service early on Easter Sunday. They gather together outside to watch the sun come up as a symbol of hope for the future.

Easter Sunday is a holiday in many countries. People give each other cards and gifts of eggs. In many parts of the world, Easter eggs are made out of chocolate. In some countries they are beautifully decorated hens' eggs.

Easter egg hunts are a popular tradition on Easter Sunday. In towns and villages in Europe, Australia and the USA, the Easter bunny hides eggs for children to find.

How to decorate Easter eggs

You can give these colourful eggs as Easter gifts, or arrange them in a basket as pretty Easter decorations.

You will need:
* newspaper
* kitchen paper
* 3 teaspoons white vinegar
* food colourings
* eggs (either hard-boiled or blown) and egg box
* rubber bands
* 250ml water

Instructions

1 Cover a work surface in thick newspaper. Place the kitchen paper on top of the newspaper.

Pour the vinegar on to the kitchen paper. Drip on some food colouring.

2 Fold the kitchen paper around an egg. Put the rubber bands around the paper to hold it in place. Pour on some water.

3 Repeat steps 1 and 2 with more kitchen paper and eggs.

4 Put the eggs in the egg box to dry overnight.

5 Take off the paper to reveal the pattern.

Fabergé eggs

In 1885, the Russian emperor asked a Russian jeweller called Peter Carl Fabergé to design a jewel-encrusted egg as an Easter present for his wife. The empress was delighted, and the tradition continued almost every Easter until 1917. Each valuable Fabergé egg is different, but they all open to reveal a secret – some have moving parts, others contain tiny paintings, sculptures, clocks or miniature ships.

19

Make an Easter flower garden

In some parts of the world many colourful spring flowers come into bloom around Easter time. This garden of flowers will last a lot longer than real ones.

You will need:
* egg box
* coloured paints/felt-tip pens
* coloured paper
* pencil
* scissors
* glue and spreader
* lolly sticks
* bottle caps
* modelling clay
* chick decoration

Instructions
Paint the egg box green – leave it to dry.

Daffodils

1 Draw a daffodil flower on a piece of yellow paper and cut it out. Draw round the shape on a second piece of paper and cut it out.

2 Glue the two pieces of paper together with a lolly stick sandwiched between them.

3 Paint the bottle cap yellow and leave it to dry. Glue the bottle cap in the centre of the flower. Glue long green petals cut from green paper to the lolly stick.

20

Tulips

1 Draw a tulip flower on a piece of coloured paper and cut it out. Draw round the shape on a second piece of paper and cut it out.

2 Glue the two pieces of paper together with the lolly stick sandwiched between them. Decorate the tulip with a funky pattern.

3 Glue long green leaves cut from green paper to the lolly stick.

Put some modelling clay into the bottom of the egg box. Push the lolly sticks into the modelling clay to make a colourful garden of spring flowers. Add a chick decoration as shown in the picture below.

Easter parades

Easter parades are held all over the world. Some are Christian festivals. Others are now just for fun.

There are Easter Day parades in cities all over the USA. The Fifth Avenue parade in New York is the most famous. People wear their best clothes and beautifully decorated hats.

This float shows Jesus after his resurrection. It is part of a religious Easter day parade in Central America.

In the past, people wore plain, dull clothes during Lent. Then, once Lent was over they decorated their hats with flowers to go to church. Today, people still wear 'Easter bonnets' on Easter Sunday.

Make an Easter chick card

You will need:
* A4-sized thin white card x 2
* scissors
* coloured felt-tip pens
* thin yellow card
* glue and spreader
* scrap of orange card
* split pin

Wish someone a 'Happy Easter' with this card. It opens up to reveal a chick.

Instructions

1 Carefully fold an A4 piece of thin card in half.

2 Cut out an egg shape from another piece of thin card. Make sure the shape will fit on the front of the card. Decorate it on one side.

3 Turn the egg shape over. Cut it in half across the middle with a zig-zag line.

4 Draw the body and head of an Easter chick on the yellow card. Cut it out.

5 Spread glue on to the back of the chick. Glue the chick on to the card. Draw on two eyes.

Cut a beak shape from the orange card. Glue it on to the head of the chick.

6 Glue the bottom half of the egg over the chick.

7 Ask an adult to fix the top of the egg on to the card with the split pin as shown.

Easter chicks

Chicks hatching are a sign of new life. Easter cards are sometimes decorated with chicks to remind people of Jesus's resurrection.

Make Easter egg nests

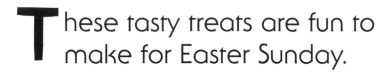

T hese tasty treats are fun to make for Easter Sunday.

Instructions

1 Break the chocolate into pieces and put them in a bowl with the butter and golden syrup.

2 Ask an adult to melt the mixture in the microwave for 30 seconds. Or get help to melt it in a bowl over a pan of boiling water.

3 Add the cornflakes to the chocolate mixture, being careful not to crush them too much.

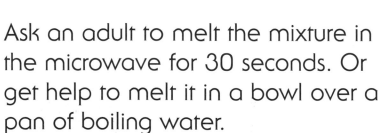

4 When the cornflakes are all coated with chocolate, spoon some of the mixture into each cake case.

Make a hollow in the middle with the back of a spoon.

5 Put the egg nests in the fridge to set.

Decorate with mini eggs and chicks.

Easter eggs

In the past, people did not eat eggs during Lent, so there were lots to use up at Easter time. Cracking open an egg reminds Christians of the empty tomb and Jesus's resurrection from the dead.

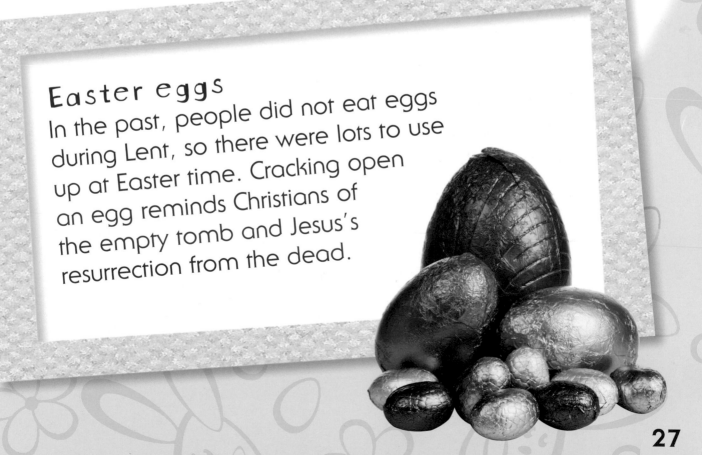

Make a rabbit-ears hat

Try making this fun rabbit-ears hat for Easter.

You will need:
* thin white card
* ruler
* pencil
* scissors
* sticky tape
* pink paper
* glue and spreader
* cotton wool

Instructions

1 Cut a strip of white card about 5cm wide. It needs to be long enough to wrap around your head and overlap by about 2cm. Use sticky tape to join the band so that it fits comfortably around your head.

2 Cut two ears out of white card each about 20cm long x 8cm wide. Cut two smaller ears out of pink paper.

3 Cover the white ears in glue and stick cotton wool on.

4 Glue the pink ears on to the centre of each cotton-wool-covered ear.

5 Glue the ears inside the band on either side of the join.

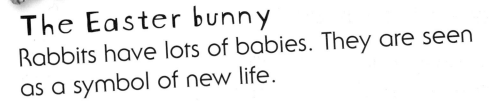

The Easter bunny

Rabbits have lots of babies. They are seen as a symbol of new life.

In some countries, the Easter bunny leaves a basket of chocolate eggs and other treats for children on Easter Sunday morning.

Glossary

arrest To seize someone by law.

Ash Wednesday The first day of Lent. It gets its name from the ashes used to make the mark of a cross on a person's forehead.

Christian A person who follows the teachings of Jesus Christ.

crucifixion An ancient method of execution. The victim was nailed or bound to a cross shape made from wood and left to die.

disciple A follower of Christ.

float In a parade or carnival, a float is a decorated platform mounted on a truck that moves slowly along the streets.

Good Friday The Friday of Holy Week when Christians believe Jesus was crucified and died.

gospel The teaching of Jesus Christ.

heaven In Christianity, the home of God, of the angels and of the good after death.

Holy Week The week leading up to Easter Sunday, which starts with Palm Sunday.

Lent The forty days before Easter, starting with Ash Wednesday.

Mardi Gras Another term for Shrove

Tuesday – in French it means 'Fat Tuesday' because it was the day that people used up all the fats and other foods they were not allowed to eat during Lent.

northern hemisphere The northern half of the Earth's surface, north of the Equator.

Palestine In Bible times, Palestine was a region on the eastern shore of the Mediterranean Sea.

palm A tree that has a crown of long, feathered leaves.

palm cross A cross made from palm leaves.

Palm Sunday The Sunday before Easter, when Jesus entered Jerusalem on a donkey.

Passover A Jewish festival that remembers the time when the Israelites (Jews) escaped from Egyptian slavery.

priest A person who carries out the sacred rites of a religion.

resurrection In Christianity, the belief that Jesus Christ rose from the dead on Easter Sunday.

Shrove Tuesday The day before Ash Wednesday.

tomb A place, often underground, for burying the dead.

Index